Covers

Christa Valentine

CAPE TOWN

To my parents with gratitude for and appreciation
of their faith and support

ACKNOWLEDGEMENTS

Formex Industries who provided the hot-glue gun
and adhesives in the photograph on p. 4 and who carried
the photographic costs.
Biggie Best who made available their shop
in the Tyger Valley Centre, Durbanville, for the photography.
Riaan Venter who sawed the hardboard for the mirrors.
Bennie Loots who cut the foam for the mirrors.
Dalene Muller of Tafelberg Publishers
for her encouragement.

© 1992 Delos

Also available in Afrikaans as *Oortreksels*

Translated by Hannetjie Gericke
Photography by Anton de Beer
Styling by Suzette Kotzé
Illustrations by André Visser
Cover design by Etienne van Duyker
Typography by Alison Stander
Typeset in 10.5 on 11pt Souvenir Light by Martingraphix, Cape Town
Printed and bound by ABC Press, Cape Town

First impression 1992

ISBN 1-86826-248-0

Contents

MATERIALS   4

BASIC TECHNIQUES   4

PROJECTS
Pink photo album for a teenager   6
Covered notebook   7
Rectangular calico picture frame   8
Frames-on-a-cord   9
Jewellery basket   10
Trinket basket   11
Large, oval-shaped mirror frame with calico frill   12
Small, oval-shaped calico frame   13
Blotter   14
Pencil holder   14
Alice band   15
Photo album with bouquet   16
Double frame   16
Small upright frame   18
Large upright frame   19
Oval-shaped mirror with floral frame   20
Rectangular floral mirror frame with lace frill   21
Sewing basket   22
Wedding album   24
Triple frame   25
Rectangular lace frame   26
Lace album   27
Diary   28
Telephone/address index book   28

Materials

Anglaise lace: As anglaise lace sometimes is too wide for a frill, it is often necessary to trim it.

Batting: Unless otherwise stated, thick batting is used.

Calico: Pre-shrunk, unbleached calico.

Cardboard: The cardboard for the projects is available from stationers. The thickness of the cardboard (1 mm or 2 mm) is indicated in the list of materials for each project.

Clear adhesive: In the text Bostik refers to Bostik clear adhesive. If no particular glue is specified in the instructions, either Bostik clear adhesive or hot glue may be used (see *Hot glue* below).

Foam: The thickness of the foam is specified in the list of materials for each project.

Hot glue: Use Bostik hot-glue sticks (see photograph) in a hot-glue gun. *Note:* Do not glue a torchon lace frill with hot glue, as the glue sets so quickly that it is not possible to adjust the frill properly. In all other instances hot glue may be substituted for Bostik clear adhesive.

Hot-glue gun: Although a hot-glue gun (see photograph) is relatively expensive, it is worth the investment if

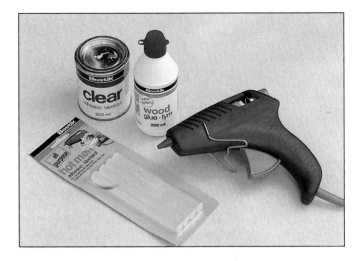

you plan to glue on a large scale, as hot glue sets immediately. However, Bostik clear adhesive works just as well.

Stanley knife: Available from hardware stores, this knife is used for all the cutting.

Wood glue: Bostik wood glue is used for the projects. The instructions specify when wood glue is required. Keep in mind that wood glue takes longer to dry in damp weather.

Basic techniques

How to cut or saw out pattern pieces

Photocopy or trace the pattern pieces on thin paper. Glue them onto the cardboard or hardboard before cutting them out. Then cut or saw out the pattern pieces along the lines.

How to cover foam or batting

Always ensure that the fabric is drawn evenly over the batting or foam while being glued. When drawing the edge of the fabric to the back and glueing, no batting should be folded to the back, as this will result in an uneven edge.

How to glue with Bostik

Bostik usually is not applied to the fabric itself, but to the surface on which the fabric is to be glued. This reduces the possibility of the glue showing through the fabric. Apply a strip of Bostik to the surface to be glued and spread it with your finger. If you have to glue an edge, for instance, spread the strip of adhesive ± 1 cm wide. Leave for about a minute to dry slightly and then glue together. If the adhesive becomes too dry, apply some more.

How to glue lace

Apply a thin zigzag line of Bostik to the lace. The Bostik

should be applied to the embroidered section of the anglaise lace to prevent it from showing on the right side.

How to glue ribbon

Apply a very thin line of Bostik to the ribbon and glue together.

How to glue piping

Apply Bostik to one side of the piping along the stitching. If the piping is glued onto a continuous edge, one end of the piping should be glued to the back of the article and taken to the edge at a slight angle until visible in front (see photograph of *Upright frame*, p. 19). Continue glueing the piping onto the edge until the starting point is reached. Take the end to the back at the same angle as before. Where applicable, always start and finish in the centre at the bottom.

How to glue edgings

Start and finish frills and lace as described above for piping, but always in the centre at the bottom, except for a rectangular frame with corners that are not rounded off.

How to glue curved corners

In the case of a frame with curved corners (see *Upright frame*, p. 19) the fabric at the side edges is first drawn to the back and glued, followed by the rest at the top and bottom edges. Then start glueing one corner where it begins to curve. Fold a knife pleat, pull the fabric taut and press down on the cardboard. Fold the next pleat directly alongside the first, pull taut and press down. Continue until the corner has been completed. Glue the other corners in the same way and trim all excess fabric.

How to make a ribbon rose

• Thread a needle with matching thread and knot the ends together.
• Fold the ribbon for the rose in half and mark the centre.
• Place the ribbon flat with the wrong side up. Cut a notch in the end on your right to mark it.
• Hold the ribbon in the centre between your left thumb and forefinger (right hand if you are left-handed), still with the wrong side facing you, and fold the right half (**R**) up (fig. 1a).
• Fold the left half (**L**) to the right (fig. 1b) and then to the back around the centre fold to lie on the left side again (fig. 1c), all the while holding the folded part firmly with the thumb.
• Fold **R** away from you and downwards. Fold **L** away from you (around the back) and to the right. Fold **R** away from you and upwards. Fold **L** away from you (around the back) and to the left.
• Repeat the four folding steps about four more times (about 20 folds in all). More folds make a fuller rose.
• Hold the two ribbons firmly at the last fold and let go of the folded part. It forms a braid. Carefully pull in the marked ribbon (**R**) while still holding the ribbons firmly. While the ribbon is pulled through, the braid is gathered and forms the rose.
• Push the needle through the ribbons at the base and twist the thread around the base a few times to form a "stem" for the rose. Push the needle up through the centre of the rose to the top and down again. Repeat three or four times and secure the thread at the bottom. Cut off the excess ribbon.

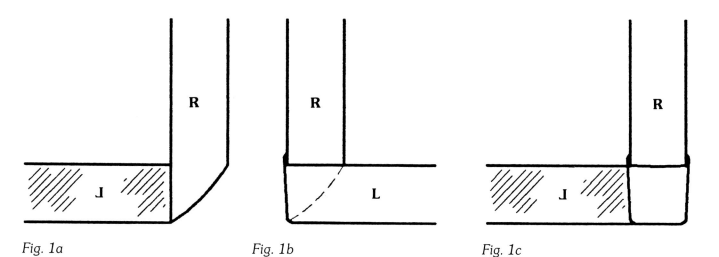

Fig. 1a   *Fig. 1b*   *Fig. 1c*

Projects

Pink photo album for a teenager *(29 cm × 30 cm)*

MATERIALS

Album
Ring-back loose-leaf album: 29 cm × 30 cm
± 1 mm-thick cardboard for flyleaves: 27 cm × 29 cm (2 pieces)
Batting: 32 cm × 65 cm
Pink cotton fabric for cover (front and back): 34 cm × 78 cm
Calico for flyleaves: 31 cm × 33 cm (2 pieces)
3 cm-wide cream anglaise lace for cover front: 1,3 m; and frill around cover: 4,5 m
4 cm-wide cream anglaise lace for spine: 34 cm
3,5 cm-wide cream ribbon to tie album: 1,25 m
Cream satin piping for outside edge: 2 m
Clear adhesive (Bostik)
Wood glue
Hot-glue gun and glue sticks (optional)

Frame
± 2 mm-thick cardboard: 12 cm × 14 cm
Batting: 12 cm × 14 cm
Pink cotton fabric: 16 cm × 18 cm
1 cm-wide torchon lace for window edge: 30 cm
3 cm-wide cream anglaise lace for frill: 1 m
1 cm-wide cream ribbon for rose and bow: 1 m
Cream satin piping: 1 m
Stanley knife

METHOD

Cover
• With Bostik, glue the batting onto the entire cover of the album and trim the edges.
• Fold open the album and place the cover with the batting down in the centre on the wrong side of the piece of cotton fabric. Apply Bostik to the inside along the short sides of the cover with batting, fold the fabric to the wrong side and glue together.
• Repeat with the long sides. Also glue the double layer at the corners. Lift the end of the metal strip in the centre of the album and push the fabric underneath with a knife with a rounded point.
• Cut two 3 cm-wide 30 cm anglaise strips and two 35 cm anglaise strips.
• With Bostik, glue the lace first to the two short and then to the two long sides of the cover front (see photograph). Trim the ends of the short lace strips flush with the edge. Fold and glue the raw edges and the ends of the long lace strips to the inside. Note that the raw edge of the lace next to the spine folds over onto the spine.

• Fold the raw edge of the anglaise lace for the spine 1 cm to the wrong side and glue the lace onto the spine so that the embroidered edge faces towards the cover front (see photograph). Fold the ends to the inside and push them under the metal strip.
• Glue the piping on the inside onto the outside edge of the album. Start and finish in the centre of the lower end of the spine.
• Gather the anglaise lace for the frill.
• Apply Bostik at the back to the piping on the inside edge of the cover. Start at the same place as for the piping and glue on the lace frill all round section by section (see photograph).

Flyleaves
• Place a piece of cardboard in the centre of a piece of calico. Apply Bostik to the edge of the cardboard, fold the calico to the back and glue first the two long and then the two short sides. Repeat with the other piece of cardboard and calico.
• Apply wood glue at the back to the two short but only one long side of the flyleaves. (The long side next to the spine is not glued.)
• Cut the 3,5 cm-wide ribbon in half. Place the end of one ribbon on the inside on the edge of the cover front so that the other end lies to the outside.
• Glue a flyleaf with the outside up in position on the inside of the cover front.
• Glue the other flyleaf and ribbon to the inside of the cover back, following the above method.
• Clamp the outer edges with clothes-pegs for ± 3 hours.

Frame
• Cut the frame panel (fig. 7a) out of the cardboard using the Stanley knife.
• With Bostik, glue batting onto one side (the front) of the frame panel.
• Place the rest of the batting on top and trim the edges flush with the outside edge of the frame panel.
• Cut out the batting flush with the inside edge (at the window) of the frame panel.
• Place the frame panel with the batting down on the wrong side in the centre of the pink cotton fabric.
• Apply Bostik around the outside edge of the frame panel.
• Press the cardboard down firmly on the batting and fabric with one hand by spreading five fingers evenly around the window. With the other hand fold the fabric along one edge to the back. Glue together.
• Repeat with the other long edge and the two short edges.
• Glue the four corners neatly (see p. 5).
• Push back any batting protruding beyond the edge of the window with your finger.
• Cut out the fabric all round 1 cm from the window.

• In the fabric edge around the window cut notches ± 1 cm apart up to the cardboard edge. Push the batting back between the fabric and the cardboard, pressing together where you are cutting.
• Apply Bostik at the back around the window. Fold the notched fabric edge to the back section by section and glue.
• Cut a 50 cm length of satin piping.
• With Bostik glue it onto the outside edge on the back of the frame.
• Cut notches ± 1 cm apart along one edge of the torchon lace.
• Apply a thin line of Bostik in front on one half of the window edge.
• Wipe the glue off towards the back with your finger, leaving a very thin layer. Be very careful not to allow any glue to run to the front.
• Glue the torchon lace onto the edge of the window, allowing the notched edge to fold round to the back.
• Repeat with the other half of the window edge.
• Apply Bostik to the back around the window and glue on the notched edge of the torchon lace.
• Cut a 30 cm length of satin piping and with Bostik glue it onto the edge of the window.
• Gather the anglaise lace for the frill.
• Apply Bostik at the back to the piping on the outside edge and glue on the gathered edge of the lace frill section by section.
• Glue the frame onto the front of the album with wood glue (see photograph) and place under a weight (e.g. two heavy books) for ± 3 hours to dry.
• Make a ribbon rose (see p. 5) and bow, and glue them into position with Bostik or hot glue (see photograph).

Covered notebook

MATERIALS

Hard-cover notebook: 9 cm × 13 cm
Pink cotton fabric: 15 cm × 20 cm
Thin batting: 9 cm × 13 cm
1,5 cm-wide anglaise lace with pink embroidered edge: 15 cm
Clear adhesive (Bostik)

METHOD

• With Bostik glue the batting onto the front and trim the edges.
• Fold open the book and place the cover with the batting downwards in the centre on the wrong side of the cotton fabric. Apply Bostik to the short sides of the cover, fold the fabric to the inside and glue together. Loosen the bound pages of the book slightly at the top and bottom of the spine to be able to push the fabric underneath.
• Apply Bostik to the entire length of the long sides, fold the fabric to the inside and glue together.
• Fold the long raw edge of the anglaise lace 1 cm to the wrong side and with Bostik glue the lace onto the spine, the embroidered edge facing forward (see photograph). Push the top and bottom ends underneath the loosened pages.
• Make flyleaves by glueing the first and last pages of the book to the inside of the front and back covers.

Rectangular calico picture frame *(24,5 cm × 36 cm)*

This frame is made of hardboard and filled with foam. Ask your dealer to saw out the hardboard for you. First draw the window (15,5 cm × 27 cm) on the board and add a 4,5 cm edge all round. Place a round spice bottle on the corners of the frame and back panel as well as the window to obtain the correct curve.

MATERIALS

Hardboard: 24,5 cm × 36 cm (2 pieces)
2 cm-thick foam: 24,5 cm × 36 cm
Calico for frame panel: 34 cm × 45 cm (2 pieces); and back panel: 30 cm × 40 cm
Cream taffeta for lower bow: 15 cm × 52 cm; top bow: 9 cm × 22 cm; and band of bow: 4 cm × 10 cm
2,5 cm-wide torchon lace for edge of window: 1 m
4 cm-wide cream anglaise lace for outside frill: 2,5 m
2,5 cm-wide cream anglaise lace for inside frill: 2,5 m
Cream satin piping: 2,2 m
8 screws: 6 mm × 16 mm
2 screw-in hooks for chain
Chain: 20 cm
Clear adhesive (Bostik)
Hot-glue gun and glue sticks (optional)
Screwdriver
Stanley knife

METHOD

• Saw or have the hardboard sawn for the frame and back panel (see p. 4).

Frame panel
• Cut the foam according to the frame panel using the Stanley knife.
• With Bostik glue the foam onto the rough side of the frame panel.
• Place the frame panel with the foam down in the centre of the calico. Apply Bostik at the back to the long and short sides of the frame panel, fold the calico over and glue onto the back.
• Neatly glue the four corners (see p. 5).
• Cut out the calico 3 cm from the window all round.
• Cut notches 2 cm apart up to the cardboard edge in the calico edge around the window. Press the calico and foam together on the edge where you are cutting.
• Apply Bostik at the back around the window. Fold the notched calico edge to the back, section by section and glue together. Pay special attention to the corners.
• Cover the frame panel in exactly the same way with the second piece of calico.
• With Bostik glue the torchon lace onto one half of the window edge, so that one edge folds to the back. Glue the other half.

• Apply Bostik at the back around the window and glue on the lace that was folded back.
• Cut a 70 cm piece of satin piping and glue it at the back onto the edge of the window.
• Glue the rest of the piping onto the outside edge of the frame panel.
• Gather the 2,5 cm-wide anglaise frill.
• Glue the frill section by section (± 20 cm at a time) onto the outside edge of the frame panel, using a thick line of glue.
• Repeat with the 4 cm-wide anglaise lace for the outside frill.

Back panel
• Using the same method as for the frame panel, cover the back panel with calico. Apply the glue to the smooth side of the hardboard.

Double bow
• Fold one long edge of the taffeta for the band to the wrong side three times, 1 cm at a time, press and glue each fold.
• Fold the taffeta for the lower bow in half lengthways with the right sides together and stitch the edges together with a 0,5 cm seam allowance, but leave an opening in the long edge to turn the strip right side out. Stitch the corners at a slight curve.
• Turn the strip right side out and press so that the seam lies next to the fold.
• Fold the strip in half with the short edges and the wrong sides together. Stitch through all layers parallel to the short sides 13 cm from the fold.
• Fold the strip flat (see fig. 2).
• Fold the taffeta for the top bow in half lengthways with the right sides together and stitch the long edges with a 0,5 cm seam allowance.
• Turn the strip right side out and press so that the seam lies next to the fold.
• Fold the strip in half with the short edges and the wrong sides together and stitch the short edge with a 0,5 cm seam allowance.
• Fold the strip so that the seam is in the centre at the back.
• Place the top bow in the centre on top of the lower bow. Make three folds in the centre of both bows to form a double bow.
• Place the band around the folds and stitch it at the back with a double thread of matching cotton. Trim the excess fabric.
• Pull the two free ends of the bow into position (see photograph).

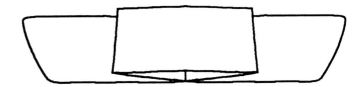

Fig. 2

Finishing

• Place the back panel with the uncovered side onto the back of the frame panel.

• Mark the positions for the screws 1,5 cm from the edge: three holes evenly spaced on each long side and one in the centre of each short side.

• Carefully drill holes at the marks through the calico and hardboard and screw the panels together.

• Carefully drill holes for the hooks for the chain in the back panel 3 cm from the long edges and 3 cm from the top edge, screw in the hooks and hook in the chain.

• With Bostik glue the bow into position (see photograph).

Frames-on-a-cord

MATERIALS (for 1 frame)

± 2 mm-thick cardboard: 12 cm × 14 cm (2 pieces)
Batting: 12 cm × 14 cm (2 pieces)
Calico for frame and back panel: 16 cm × 18 cm
    (2 pieces); back panel: 9 cm × 11 cm; long cord:
    11 cm × 54 cm; bow: 11 cm × 25 cm; and band for
    bow: 4 cm × 8 cm
1 cm-wide torchon lace for edge of window: 30 cm
2,5 cm-wide anglaise lace for frill: 1,25 m
1 cm-wide cream satin ribbon for rose: 1,5 m
Cream satin piping for edge of window: 30 cm; outside

edge of frame panel: 50 cm; and outside edge of back
    panel: 50 cm
2 artificial leaves
Clear adhesive (Bostik)
Wood glue
Hot-glue gun and glue sticks (optional)
Stanley knife

METHOD

Frame

• Cut the frame and back panel (fig. 7a) out of the cardboard using the Stanley knife.

• With Bostik glue the batting onto one side (the front) of the frame panel.

• Place the other piece of batting on top and trim the edges flush with the outside edge of the frame panel.

• Cut out the batting flush with the inside edge (at the window) of the frame panel.

• Place the frame panel with the batting side down in the centre of a 16 cm × 18 cm piece of calico. Apply Bostik to the outside edge at the back of the frame panel.

• Press the cardboard down firmly on the batting and fabric with one hand by spreading five fingers evenly around the window edge. With the other hand fold the fabric along one long edge to the back. Glue together.

• Repeat with the other long edge and then with the two short edges. Neatly glue the four corners (see p. 5).

• Push back any batting protruding beyond the edge of the window with your finger.

- Cut out the calico all round 1 cm from the window.
- Cut notches ± 1 cm apart in the calico edge around the window up to the cardboard edge. Push the batting back between the calico and the cardboard, pressing down where you are cutting.
- Apply Bostik at the back around the window. Fold the notched calico edge back section by section and glue together.
- Glue the satin piping along the outside edge on the back of the frame.
- Cut notches ± 1 cm apart in one edge of the torchon lace.
- Apply a thin line of Bostik in front on one half of the window edge. Wipe off the excess glue towards the back with your finger, leaving only a very thin layer. Be very careful not to allow any glue to run to the front.
- Glue the torchon lace onto one half of the window edge, so that the notched edge folds round to the back.
- Repeat with the other half of the window edge.
- Apply Bostik at the back around the window and glue on the notched edge of the torchon lace.
- With Bostik glue the piping at the back onto the window edge. Gather the anglaise lace for the frill.
- Apply Bostik at the back to the piping on the outside edge and glue on the gathered edge of the lace frill section by section.
- Place the cardboard for the back panel in the centre of the remaining 16 cm × 18 cm piece of calico. Glue the edge of the fabric onto the back as described for the frame panel and trim the excess fabric.
- Apply Bostik on the back of the back panel next to the edge of the fabric. Glue on the 9 cm × 11 cm piece of calico and smooth the fabric with your fingers until taut.
- Glue piping at the back onto edge of the back panel.
- Apply wood glue at the back to the sides of the frame panel. Glue the frame panel onto the wrong side of the back panel and clamp for 3-4 hours with clothes-pegs.
- Make a ribbon rose (see p. 5). Glue the leaves to the frame (see photograph) and glue the ribbon rose on top.

Long cord
- Fold the calico for the cord in half lengthways and stitch the long edges with a 0,5 cm seam allowance.
- Turn the strip right side out and press so that the seam lies next to the fold.
- Fold one end (the lower end) 1 cm to the wrong side, press and glue.
- Fold each of the two corners of the lower edge to the wrong side at an angle of 45° so that the lower edge forms a sharp point (see photograph). Press. Apply glue to the 1 cm hem and glue the corners onto the back.
- Fold the top edge of the cord to the wrong side twice, 0,5 cm at a time, press and glue each fold.
- Fold the two long edges to the wrong side at the top to meet in the centre of the top edge. Fold open, apply glue to the inside (wrong side) of the two corners and press down as it was folded.

Single bow
- Fold one long edge of the calico for the band over three times, 1 cm at a time, press and glue each fold.

- Fold the calico for the bow in half lengthways with right sides together and stitch the long edges together with a 0,5 cm seam allowance.
- Turn the strip right side out and press it so that the seam lies next to the fold.
- Fold the strip in half with the short edges and the wrong sides together. Stitch the short edges with a 0,5 cm seam allowance.
- Fold the strip so that the seam is in the centre at the back.
- Gather the strip in the centre into three folds to form a bow.
- Place the band around the folds and stitch at the back with a double thread of matching cotton. Trim the excess fabric.

Finishing
- With Bostik glue the bow in front to the top end of the cord.
- Space the frames along the cord and glue on with Bostik.
- Hook the top end of the cord over a picture hook to hang.

Jewellery basket

Any shape and size basket with a loose lid can be covered according to the instructions. Cut the cardboard for the top according to the shape of the lid and adjust the materials.

MATERIALS

Oval-shaped basket with loose lid: 10 cm × 15 cm
± 1 mm-thick cardboard: 10 cm × 15 cm
Batting: 10 cm × 15 cm
Floral cotton fabric: 15 cm × 20 cm
Pink cotton piping: 50 cm
10 cm-wide cream anglaise lace with pink embroidery: 2 m
8 mm-wide pink satin ribbon: 60 cm
Clear adhesive (Bostik)
Wood glue
Hot-glue gun and glue sticks (optional)
Stanley knife

METHOD

- Trace the outside edge of the lid on the cardboard and cut out using the Stanley knife.
- Cut out the batting according to the cardboard.
- Place the cardboard on the floral fabric, add 2 cm all round and cut out.
- With Bostik glue the batting onto the cardboard.
- Place the cardboard with the batting down in the centre on the wrong side of the floral fabric. Apply Bostik at

the back to the edge of the cardboard, fold the fabric to the back and glue together. Make small folds in the fabric at the curves.

• With Bostik glue the piping at the back onto the edge of the covered cardboard.

• Cut a 1,25 m strip of anglaise lace for the frill of the lid. Trim the lace to a width of 6 cm and gather.

• With Bostik glue the gathered edge of the lace frill at the back onto the piping along the edge of the covered cardboard. First glue one half of the edge and then the rest.

• Cut a 42 cm strip of anglaise lace for the side of the basket.

• Fold the raw edge to the wrong side so that the lace is just wide enough to cover the side of the basket that shows below the edge of the lid.

• Apply a zigzag strip of Bostik to the side of the basket. Start at a narrow end of the basket and glue on the lace.

• Cut a 42 cm piece of ribbon and with Bostik glue it onto the fold of the lace. Start and finish at the same point as for the lace.

• Make a ribbon bow and glue it onto the end of the glued ribbon with Bostik.

• Start at the edge and apply four circles of wood glue to the top of the lid.

• Place the covered cardboard on the lid, place a weight (e.g. three heavy books) on top and leave for ± 3 hours.

Trinket basket

MATERIALS

Oval-shaped basket with loose lid: 11 cm × 8 cm
± 1 mm-thick cardboard: 12 cm × 10 cm

Batting: 12 cm × 10 cm
Floral cotton fabric: 15 cm × 12 cm
Pink cotton piping: 32 cm
3,5 cm-wide cream anglaise lace with pink embroidery: 1 m
Clear adhesive (Bostik)
Wood glue
Hot-glue gun and glue sticks (optional)
Stanley knife

METHOD

• Trace the outside edge of the lid on the cardboard and cut out using the Stanley knife.

• Cut the batting according to the cardboard.

• Place the cardboard on the floral fabric, add 2 cm all round and cut out.

• With Bostik glue the batting onto the cardboard.

• Place the cardboard with the batting down in the centre on the wrong side of the floral fabric. Apply Bostik at the back to the edge of the cardboard, fold the fabric to the back and glue together. Make small folds in the fabric along the curves.

• With Bostik glue the piping at the back onto the edge of the covered cardboard.

• Gather the anglaise lace to fit around the lid of the basket.

• With Bostik glue the gathered edge of the lace frill onto the piping at the back along the edge of the covered cardboard. First glue one half of the edge and then the rest.

• Start at the edge and apply four circles of wood glue to the top of the lid.

• Glue the covered cardboard on the cover, place a weight (e.g. three heavy books) on top and leave for ± 3 hours.

Large, oval-shaped mirror frame with calico frill

To obtain the correct shape for the mirror, trace the outline of the window (see Method) on cardboard, add ± 2 cm all round and cut out. Ask your dealer to cut your mirror accordingly.

MATERIALS

Mirror: 45 cm × 55 cm
3 mm-thick hardboard: 45 cm × 55 cm (2 pieces)
2 cm-thick foam: 45 cm × 55 cm
Calico for frame and back panel: 45 cm × 55 cm (3 pieces); frill: 14 cm × 3 m; top bow: 14 cm × 30 cm; lower bow: 1,2 m × 25 cm; and band for bow: 8 cm × 15 cm
3 cm-wide torchon lace for window: 1 m
5 cm-wide torchon lace for inner frill: 4 m
1,5 cm-wide torchon lace for calico frill: 3 m
Cream satin piping: 2,55 m
8 screws: 6 mm × 16 mm
Chain: 25 cm
2 screw-in hooks for chain
4 squares 2 mm-thick double-sided mirror tape
Clear adhesive (Bostik)
Hot-glue gun and glue sticks (optional)
Drill with 1,8 mm bit
Screwdriver
Tracing paper (optional)

METHOD

• Photocopy or trace the pattern for the frame (fig. 5) onto paper. Make two copies following the solid lines and two following the broken lines. Do not cut out the pattern – glue it onto the hardboard and have it sawn out. Saw the back panel according to the frame panel.

Frame panel
• Cut out the foam according to the frame panel.
• With Bostik glue the foam onto the rough side of the frame panel.
• Place the frame panel with the foam down in the centre of a 45 cm × 55 cm piece of calico.
• Apply Bostik at the back along the outside edge of the frame panel, fold back the calico and glue together. Make small folds in the calico at the curves and trim the excess calico.
• Cut out the calico all round 3 cm from the window.
• Cut notches ± 2 cm apart up to the hardboard edge in the calico edge around the window.
• Press the foam and calico together onto the edge where you are cutting.
• Apply Bostik at the back around the window. Fold the notched calico edge back section by section and glue onto the back.

• Cover the frame panel with another layer of calico in exactly the same way.
• Glue the 3 cm-wide torchon lace in front on half of the window edge so that one edge folds round to the back. Repeat with the other half of the window edge.
• Apply Bostik at the back around the window and glue on the edge of the torchon lace.
• Cut a 1 m piece of satin piping and with Bostik glue it at the back round the window edge.
• Glue the remaining piping onto the outside edge.
• Gather the 5 cm-wide torchon lace.
• Apply Bostik to the wrong side of the piping along the edge.
• Start at the bottom in the centre and glue on the lace frill section by section (± 20 cm at a time).

Calico frill
• Fold the calico for the frill in half lengthways with the two long edges corresponding exactly and stitch the long edges with a 0,5 cm seam allowance.
• Place the 1,5 cm-wide torchon lace with the right side at the back against the fold of the calico strip and stitch.
• Gather the other long edge of the calico strip.
• Apply Bostik or hot glue at the back onto the gathered edge of the torchon lace frill along the outside edge and glue on the calico frill section by section (± 20 cm at a time).

Back panel
• Place the hardboard for the back panel with the smooth side up in the centre of the calico.
• Apply Bostik to the hardboard and glue the calico edge onto the back as described for the frame panel. Trim the excess fabric.

Double bow
• Fold one long edge of the calico for the band to the wrong side three times, 2 cm at a time, press and glue each fold.
• Follow the rest of the instructions for the double bow of *Rectangular calico picture frame* on p. 8 (replace taffeta with calico), but stitch through all layers parallel to the short sides 22 cm (instead of 13 cm) from the fold.

Finishing
• Cut the mirror tape squares in half. Place two pieces in the centre at the back of the mirror and arrange the rest around the edge.
• Place the mirror in position on the back of the back panel and press it down onto the mirror tape.
• Place the back panel with the mirror side down on the back of the frame panel.
• Mark the positions for eight evenly spaced screws 1,5 cm from the edge on the back panel. Carefully drill holes at the marks through the calico and hardboard and screw the panels together.
• Carefully drill holes for the hooks in the back panel 3 cm from the long edges and 3 cm from the top edge, screw in the hooks and hook in the chain.
• Glue the bow into position with Bostik or hot glue (see photograph).

Small, oval-shaped calico frame

MATERIALS

Frame *(for 1 frame)*
3 mm-thick hardboard: 30 cm × 25 cm (2 pieces)
2 cm-thick foam: 30 cm × 25 cm
Calico for frame and back panel: 30 cm × 25 cm (2 pieces); bow: 12 cm × 38 cm; and band of bow: 4 cm × 8 cm
2,5 cm-wide torchon lace for frill: 1,5 m
1 cm-wide torchon lace for edge of window: 50 cm
Cream satin piping for edge of window: 50 cm; and outside edge: 75 cm
4 screws: 6 mm × 16 mm
Clear adhesive (Bostik)
Hot-glue gun and glue sticks (optional)
Drill with 1,8 mm bit
Screwdriver
Tracing paper (optional)

Long cord with bow *(for 1 cord and 1 bow)*
Calico for cord: 14 cm × 56 cm; bow: 16 cm × 32 cm; and band for bow: 4 cm × 8 cm
5 mm-wide torchon lace: 1,15 m

METHOD

• Photocopy or trace the pattern for the frame (fig. 6) onto paper, glue it onto the hardboard and saw out the frame panel.

Frame panel
• Cut out the foam according to the frame panel.
• With Bostik glue the foam onto the rough side of the frame panel.

• Place the frame panel with the foam side down in the centre of the calico. Apply Bostik along the edge of the hardboard.
• Press the hardboard down firmly onto the foam and calico with one hand by spreading five fingers evenly around the window edge. With the other hand fold the calico to the back along one long edge. Glue together.
• Repeat with the other long edge and then with the two short edges.
• Neatly glue the four corners (see p. 5).
• Cut out the calico all round 2,5 cm from the window.
• Cut notches ± 2,5 cm apart up to the hardboard edge in the calico edge around the window. Press the calico and foam together onto the edge where you are cutting.
• Apply Bostik at the back around the window.
• Fold the notched calico edge back and glue together section by section.
• Glue the satin piping along the outside edge onto the back of the frame panel.
• Cut notches ± 1 cm apart in one edge of the torchon lace for the window edge.
• Apply a thin line of Bostik in front along one half of the window edge. Wipe the glue off towards the back with your finger, leaving a very thin layer. Be very careful not to allow any glue to run to the front.
• Glue the torchon lace onto one half of the window edge so that the notched edge folds round to the back. Repeat with the other half.
• Apply Bostik at the back around the window and glue on the notched edge of the torchon lace.
• With Bostik glue the satin piping at the back onto the window edge. Gather the torchon lace for the frill.
• Apply Bostik at the back to the piping along the outside edge and glue on the gathered edge of the lace frill.
• Place the hardboard for the back panel with the smooth side up in the centre of the remaining piece of calico. Apply Bostik to the smooth side and glue the calico edge onto the back, as described for the frame panel. Trim the excess calico.

Long cord
• Follow the instructions for the long cord of *Frames-on-a-cord* on p. 10.
• Glue or stitch lace at the back onto the edge of the cord.

Single bow
• Make one bow to glue onto the frame (according to instructions for the bow of *Photo album with bouquet* on p. 16) and another for the top end of the long cord (according to instructions for the single bow of *Frames-on-a-cord* on p. 10).

Finishing
• Place the back panel with the unfinished side down onto the back of the frame panel. Mark the positions for four evenly spaced screws 1,5 cm from the edge on the back panel. Carefully drill holes at the marks through the calico and hardboard and screw the panels together.
• Glue the frame into position on the long cord.
• Glue the bows into position with Bostik or hot glue (see photograph).
• Hook the top of the cord over a picture hook to hang the frame.

Blotter

MATERIALS

3 mm-thick hardboard: 35 cm × 56 cm
2 mm-thick cardboard: 35 cm × 56 cm
Thin batting: 35 cm × 56 cm
Floral cotton fabric: 39 cm × 60 cm
Plain pink fabric for corner strips: 12 cm × 28 cm (4 pieces)
5 cm-wide torchon lace for corners: 1 m
Clear adhesive (Bostik)
Hot-glue gun and glue sticks (optional)
Wood glue

METHOD

• With Bostik glue the batting onto the rough side of the hardboard.
• Trim the edges of the batting flush with the hardboard, if necessary.
• Place the hardboard with the batting down in the centre on the wrong side of the floral fabric. Apply Bostik to the two short sides of the hardboard. Fold fabric over and glue to the back. Ensure that fabric on the front is smooth.
• Glue the fabric of the two long sides onto the back in the same way. Slightly fold in the fabric at the corners.
• Fold one long side of a piece of pink fabric 1 cm to the wrong side and iron the fold.
• Place the pink fabric diagonally across the corner (see photograph) of the covered hardboard so that the centre of the long raw edge is exactly at the corner (see fig. 3). Fold both ends to the back and glue.

• Glue the remaining pieces of pink fabric onto the three remaining corners in the same way.
• Cut the lace for the corners into four equal strips. Apply Bostik to the most densely woven section of the lace and glue onto the pink fabric at the corner (see photograph).
• Repeat with the three remaining corners.
• Cover the cardboard with the pink fabric in the same way as the hardboard.
• Apply wood glue to the back of the hardboard and glue it to the covered cardboard with the wrong sides together.

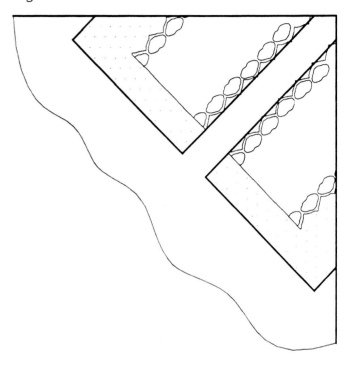

Fig. 3

Pencil holder

A plastic pill bottle was used to make the pencil holder, but any container will be suitable. Simply adjust the amount of fabric, lace and piping, if necessary.

MATERIALS

Round plastic holder: 5 cm in diameter and 10 cm high
Cotton fabric: 16 cm × 16 cm
Matching cotton piping: 16 cm
3 cm-wide cream anglaise lace: 16 cm
Clear adhesive (Bostik)

METHOD

• Fold one edge of the fabric 0,5 cm to the wrong side.

• Apply Bostik to the outside of the bottle. Glue the fabric around the bottle so that the raw edges are at the top and bottom. The bottom raw edge must be flush with the base of the bottle. Glue the folded edge last.
• Apply glue to the inside edge of the bottle, fold the fabric to the inside and glue together.
• Glue piping on the inside onto the edge of the bottle.
• Fold the long raw edge of the lace 0,5 cm to the wrong side. Glue the lace around the bottle so that the folded edge is flush with the base of the bottle (see photograph). Fold the end to the wrong side and glue.

Alice band

This Alice band measures 40 cm from end to end. Adjust the amount of fabric, foam and bias binding according to the size of your Alice band.

MATERIALS

Alice band

Floral cotton fabric: 6 cm × 40 cm (cut on the bias)
Matching bias binding: 40 cm
2 mm-thick foam or thick batting: 6 cm × 40 cm
Clear adhesive (Bostik)
Pink cotton fabric for bow: 16 cm × 4 cm; band for bow: 2,5 cm × 1,5 cm

METHOD

• Glue the foam or batting onto the outside of the Alice band and trim the edges flush with those of the band.
• Apply Bostik to the entire inside of the band. Work from the centre of the band towards the ends, glueing the fabric to both sides of the band simultaneously. Fold it to the inside at the ends and glue together.
• Apply Bostik to the raw edges of the fabric on the inside of the band. Fold under the end of the bias binding and glue it to the glued raw edges. Fold the other end under too and glue.
• Make the bow following the instructions for the single bow of *Frames-on-a-cord* on p. 10.
• With Bostik glue the bow onto the Alice band (see photograph).

Photo album with bouquet

MATERIALS

Standard-size ten-page ring-back album
± 1 mm-thick cardboard for flyleaves: 22 cm × 28,5 cm (2 pieces)
Thick batting: 32 cm × 52 cm
Thin batting: 34 cm × 36 cm
Calico for cover: 34 cm × 58 cm; flyleaves: 24 cm × 34 cm (2 pieces); and cover front: 34 cm × 36 cm
Fabric with bouquet motif: 34 cm × 36 cm
Pink cotton fabric for bow: 10 cm × 40 cm; and band of bow: 1,5 cm × 4 cm
2 cm-wide cream anglaise lace for cover front and spine: 1,6 m
2 cm-wide cream anglaise lace for frill: 2,5 m
3,5 cm-wide cream satin ribbon: 1,25 m
Pink satin piping: 1,65 m
Clear adhesive (Bostik)
Wood glue
Hot-glue gun and glue sticks (optional)

METHOD

Cover
• With Bostik glue the thick batting to the cover of the album and trim the edges.
• Open the album and place the cover with the batting down in the centre of the calico for the cover. Apply Bostik to the short sides of the cover with batting, fold the calico to the back and glue onto the inside.
• Repeat with the long sides, including the double layer at the corners.
• Place the thin batting on the calico for the cover front and place the bouquet motif with the right side up on top. Baste into position and quilt around the edge of the motif (optional).
• Place the lined bouquet motif right side down and place the cover front of the album in position on top. Ensure that the top of the motif corresponds with that of the album.
• Apply Bostik to the long side on the inside of the cover front, fold the fabric of the bouquet motif to the back and glue together.
• Repeat with the short sides. There will be three fabric layers at the corners.
• Cut two 25 cm anglaise lace strips for the cover front and glue it with Bostik onto the top and bottom edge (short sides) so that the raw edges fold to the inside. Trim the ends flush with the sides.
• Cut two 35 cm strips of the same anglaise lace and glue onto the two long sides of the cover front in the same way. The raw edge of the lace next to the spine folds over onto the spine. Fold the top and bottom end of the lace over and glue to the inside.
• Fold the long raw edge of the remaining lace to the wrong side and glue the lace onto the spine with Bostik so that the embroidered edge faces towards the cover front. The embroidered edge hides the raw edge of the lace strip on the cover front.
• Fold the top and bottom end of the lace to the inside and glue.
• Glue the piping on the inside along the outside edge. Start and finish in the centre of the lower edge of the spine.
• Gather the anglaise lace for the frill.
• Apply Bostik at the back to the piping on the outside edge. Start at the same place as for the piping and glue the gathered edge of the lace frill onto the piping section by section (see photograph).

Flyleaves
• Make the flyleaves and glue them into position with the ribbons, following the instructions for the flyleaves of *Pink photo album for a teenager* on p. 6.

Bow
• Fold one long edge of the fabric for the band over twice, 0,5 cm at a time, press and glue each fold.
• Fold the fabric for the bow in half lengthways with the right sides together. Stitch the long edges together with a 0,5 cm seam allowance, leaving an opening to turn the strip right side out. Stitch the corners at a slight curve.
• Turn the strip right side out and press so that the seam lies next to the fold.
• Fold the strip in half with the short edges and wrong sides together. Stitch 10,5 cm from the fold through all layers parallel to the short sides.
• Fold the strip flat (see fig. 2, p. 8).
• Gather the strip into three folds in the centre to form a bow.
• Place the band around the folds and stitch it at the back with a double thread of matching cotton. Trim the excess fabric.
• Pull the two free ends of the bow into position and glue the bow onto the album (see photograph).
• Apply Bostik to the back of the band and glue the bow into position on the cover front (see photograph).

Double frame

MATERIALS

± 2 mm-thick cardboard for frame and back panel: 14 cm × 17 cm (4 pieces)
Thin batting: 16 cm × 19 cm
Thick batting: 16 cm × 19 cm
Pink ticking for cover: 20 cm × 32 cm
Calico for frame panel: 20 cm × 22 cm
Pink cotton fabric for back panel: 9 cm × 11 cm; centre strip: 4 cm × 19 cm; bow on frame: 7,5 cm × 18 cm; and band for bow: 1,5 cm × 4 cm
Pink fabric with motif for second frame: 18 cm × 20 cm
5 cm-wide cream anglaise lace with pink embroidery for frame panels: 1,6 m
6 mm-wide pink satin ribbon: 1,2 m

Pink cotton piping: 1,2 m
Clear adhesive (Bostik)
Wood glue
Hot-glue gun and glue sticks (optional)
Stanley knife

METHOD

Cover

• Place two pieces of cardboard with two long sides 1 cm apart.
• Apply Bostik to the two adjacent long sides. Glue the centre strip onto the glued sides to join the pieces of cardboard. Ensure that the cardboard does not shift.
• Apply a small amount of Bostik at the back to the top and bottom where the pieces are joined. Fold over the ends of the centre strip and glue to the back.
• Place the two joined pieces of cardboard with the centre strip up on the wrong side of the pink ticking. Ensure that the outside edge is an equal distance all round from the edge of the fabric. Apply Bostik to the long sides (top and bottom), fold the fabric to the inside and glue together.
• Apply Bostik to the two short sides, fold the corners of the fabric in slightly, and glue the fabric edge to the inside.
• Apply Bostik to the cardboard next to the folded fabric edge and glue on the 9 cm × 11 cm piece of pink fabric. Smooth the fabric with the fingers until taut.
• Cut a 40 cm length of ribbon and glue it all round the spine with Bostik. Start and finish on the outside in the centre of the spine.

Frame panel

• Follow the first ten steps for the frame panel of *Triple frame* on p. 25.
• Cut two 22 cm strips and two 18 cm strips of anglaise lace. Glue the lace in front along the two short sides and trim the ends flush with the edge. Fold the raw edges over and glue to the back. Repeat with the long sides, but fold the ends and raw edges over and glue to the back. Carefully cut a small notch in the lace at each inside corner and press the lace down securely onto the edge of the window.
• Cut eight 8 cm pieces of ribbon. Glue each ribbon onto the lace (see photograph) and glue the ends at the back.
• Cut two 14 cm strips and two 11 cm strips of satin piping and glue it at the back, first on the long and then on the short window edges.

Picture panel

• Glue the thin batting onto the remaining piece of cardboard.
• Place the cardboard with the batting down in the centre on the wrong side of the fabric with the motif. Apply Bostik to the edge of the cardboard and press it down firmly onto the batting and fabric. Fold the long sides of the fabric over and glue it to the back.
• Repeat with the short sides. There will be three layers of fabric at the corners.
• Cut two 22 cm strips and two 18 cm strips of anglaise lace. With Bostik first glue the two short strips onto the short sides (see photograph). Trim the ends flush with the cardboard and glue the raw edges to the back. Repeat with the long sides, glueing the ends to the back.

- With Bostik glue the rest of the piping at the back along the outside edge.

Bow
- Fold one long side of the fabric for the band over twice, 0,5 cm at a time, press and glue each fold.
- Continue, following the rest of the instructions for the single bow of *Frames-on-a-cord* on p. 10, but replace the calico with cotton fabric.

Finishing
- Apply wood glue on the inside to three sides of the left-hand cover panel for the frame panel (not the top edge – the photograph is inserted from above).
- Place the frame panel into position and clamp for 3-4 hours using clothes pegs.
- Apply wood glue on the inside to all four sides of the right-hand cover panel for the picture panel, place the picture panel into position and clamp.
- With Bostik glue on the bow (see photograph).
- Tie the remaining ribbon in a bow and glue to the spine to hide the glued ribbon.

Small upright frame *(12 cm × 14 cm)*

MATERIALS

± 2 mm-thick cardboard for frame and back panel: 12 cm × 14 cm (2 pieces); and support: 8 cm × 12 cm (2 pieces)
Batting: 12 cm × 14 cm (2 pieces)
Calico for frame and back panel: 16 cm × 18 cm (2 pieces); back panel: 9 cm × 11 cm; and support: 8 cm × 12 cm
1,5 cm-wide torchon lace for edge of window: 30 cm
2,5 cm-wide torchon lace for frill: 1,25 m
1 cm-wide cream satin ribbon to join support to back, rose and bow: 1 m
Cream satin piping: 1,3 m
2 artificial leaves
Clear adhesive (Bostik)
Wood glue
Hot-glue gun and glue sticks (optional)
Stanley knife

METHOD

- Cut the frame and back panel (fig. 7a) out of the cardboard using the Stanley knife. Similarly cut two supports (fig. 7b) out of the cardboard, one along the broken line. The latter is the prop.

Frame
- With Bostik glue a piece of batting onto one side (the front) of the frame panel.

- Place the other batting on top and trim the edges flush with the outside edge of the frame panel.
- Cut out the batting flush with the inside edge of the frame panel (at the window).
- Place the frame panel with the batting down in the centre of a 16 cm × 18 cm piece of calico. Apply Bostik to the outside edge of the frame panel.
- Press the cardboard down firmly onto the batting and calico with one hand by spreading five fingers evenly around the window edge. With the other hand fold the calico to the back along one long edge. Glue together.
- Repeat with the other long edge and then with the two short edges. Neatly glue the corners (see p. 5).
- Push back any batting protruding beyond the cardboard along the window edge with your finger.
- Cut out the calico all round 1 cm from the window.
- Cut notches ± 1 cm apart up to the cardboard edge in the calico edge around the window. Push the batting back between the calico and the cardboard and press down where you are cutting.
- Apply Bostik at the back around the window. Fold over the notched calico edge section by section and glue to the back.
- Cut a 50 cm piece of satin piping and with Bostik glue it to the outside edge at the back of the frame.
- Cut notches ± 1 cm apart in one edge of the torchon lace for the window edge.
- Apply a thin line of Bostik in front to one half of the window edge. Wipe off the glue towards the back with your finger, leaving only a very thin layer. Be very careful not to allow any glue to run to the front.
- Glue the torchon lace onto half of the window edge so that the notched edge folds round to the back. Repeat with the other half of the edge.
- Apply Bostik at the back around the window and glue the notched edge of the torchon lace onto the back.
- Cut a 30 cm piece of satin piping and with Bostik glue it at the back onto the window edge.
- Gather the torchon lace for the frill.
- Apply Bostik at the back to the piping along the outside edge and glue on the gathered edge of the lace frill.

Back panel
- Place the cardboard for the back panel in the centre of the remaining 16 cm × 18 cm piece of calico. Glue the edge of the fabric to the back as described for the frame panel and trim all excess fabric.
- Round off the corners of the 9 cm × 11 cm piece of calico.
- Apply Bostik to the back of the back panel next to the edge of the fabric. Glue on the 9 cm × 11 cm piece of calico, smoothing the fabric with the fingers until taut.
- Glue the remaining piping at the back onto the edge of the back panel.

Support
- Cut the 8 cm × 12 cm piece of calico according to the pattern for the support adding 1 cm all round.
- Place the cardboard for the support in the centre of the calico and apply Bostik to the edge of the cardboard. Glue first the two long sides and then the two short sides

of the calico fabric to the back. Simultaneously fold the corners in slightly and neatly glue together.
• Cut a 12 cm piece of ribbon and glue one end at the back in the centre of the wide edge of the support with wood glue so that the other end lies to the outside.
• Apply wood glue to the edges of the prop and place into position on the back of the support. Clamp all round with clothes-pegs and leave to dry for ± 1 hour.
• With the Stanley knife cut into the back of the support next to the top edge of the prop. Begin and end ± 1 cm from the edge. Fold the cardboard at the incision and bend backwards and forwards until it bends easily.

Finishing
• Place the lower edge of the support on the outside of the back panel flush with and exactly in the centre of its lower edge.
• Fold the flap of the support back and with a pencil draw a circle ± 1,5 cm in diameter directly above the fold on the back panel.
• Cut the circle out of the calico along the pencil line.
• Place wood glue in the round opening on the cardboard, return the support to its exact position and press down the flap.
• Place the frame under a weight (e.g. a few heavy books) for ± 3 hours to dry.
• Glue the loose end of the ribbon at the back onto the edge of the back panel.
• Apply wood glue at the back to the piping on the back panel. Place the frame panel on the back panel and clamp for 3-4 hours with clothes pegs.
• Cut a 20 cm piece of ribbon, tie a bow and with Bostik glue it onto the fold of the support (optional).
• Make a ribbon rose (see p. 5) and glue it to the leaves on the frame (see photograph).

Large upright frame (14 cm × 18 cm)

MATERIALS

± 2 mm-thick cardboard for frame and back panel: 19 cm × 22 cm (2 pieces)
± 2 mm-thick cardboard for support: 8 cm × 12 cm (2 pieces)
Batting: 19 cm × 22 cm (2 pieces)
Calico for frame and back panel: 19 cm × 22 cm (2 pieces); back panel: 11 cm × 14 cm; and support: 8 cm × 12 cm
3 cm-wide torchon lace for frill: 2 m
1 cm-wide torchon lace for edge of window: 35 cm
1 cm-wide cream satin ribbon to join support to back: 12 cm
1,5 cm-wide cream satin ribbon for rose: 1,25 m
Cream satin piping: 1,7 m
2 artificial leaves
Clear adhesive (Bostik)
Wood glue
Hot-glue gun and glue sticks (optional)
Stanley knife

METHOD

• Complete the frame following the method for *Small upright frame* above. Cut out the frame and back panel according to fig. 7a and use the amounts of cardboard, batting, calico, lace and ribbon specified in the list of materials above.

Oval-shaped mirror with floral frame

To obtain the correct shape for the mirror, trace the outline of the window (see Method) onto cardboard, add ± 2 cm all round and cut out. Ask your dealer to cut your mirror accordingly.

MATERIALS

Mirror: 45 cm × 55 cm
3 mm-thick hardboard: 45 cm × 55 cm (2 pieces)
2 cm-thick foam: 45 cm × 55 cm
Calico for frame and back panel: 45 cm × 55 cm (2 pieces)
Floral cotton fabric for frame panel: 45 cm × 55 cm; and top bow: 14 cm × 26 cm
Pink cotton fabric for frill: 14 cm × 3 m; lower bow: 1,2 m × 25 cm; and band for bow: 8 cm × 15 cm
3 cm-wide torchon lace for window: 1 m
5 cm-wide torchon lace for inner frill: 4 m
1,5 cm-wide torchon lace for fabric frill: 3 m
Pink cotton piping: 2,55 m
8 screws: 6 mm × 16 mm
Chain: 25 cm
2 screw-in hooks for chain
4 squares 2 mm-thick double-sided mirror tape
Clear adhesive (Bostik)
Hot-glue gun and glue sticks (optional)
Drill with 1,8 mm bit
Screwdriver
Tracing paper (optional)

METHOD

• Photocopy or trace the pattern for the frame (fig. 5) onto paper. Make two copies following the solid lines and two following the broken lines. Do not cut out the pattern. Glue it onto the hardboard and have it sawn out. Saw out the back panel according to the frame panel.

Frame panel
• Cut out the foam according to the frame panel.
• With Bostik glue the foam onto the rough side of the frame panel.
• Place the frame panel with the foam down in the centre of the calico for the frame panel. Apply Bostik at the back to the outside edge of the frame panel, fold the calico edge to the back and glue together. Make small folds in the calico at the curves and trim the excess calico.
• Cut out the calico all round 3 cm from the window.
• Cut notches ± 2 cm apart up to the hardboard edge in the calico edge around the window. Press the foam and calico together on the edge where you are cutting.
• Apply Bostik at the back around the window. Fold the notched calico edge over and glue onto the back section by section.

• Cover the frame panel with the floral fabric in exactly the same way.
• With Bostik glue the 3 cm-wide torchon lace in front onto half the window edge so that one edge folds round to the back. Repeat with the other half of the window edge.
• Apply Bostik at the back around the window and glue on the edge of the torchon lace.
• Cut a 1 m piece of satin piping and with Bostik glue it at the back onto the window edge.
• Glue the remaining piping at the back along the outside edge. Gather the 5 cm-wide torchon lace.
• Apply Bostik at the back to the piping along the outside edge. Start at the bottom in the centre and glue on the lace frill section by section (± 20 cm at a time).

Pink fabric frill
• Fold the fabric for the frill in half lengthways with the wrong sides and the two long edges together. Press well. Stitch the long edges with a 0,5 cm seam allowance.
• Place the 1,5 cm-wide torchon lace with the right side behind the fold and stitch.
• Gather the other long edge of the fabric strip.
• Apply Bostik at the back to the gathered edge of the torchon lace frill on the frame panel and glue on the pink fabric frill section by section (± 20 cm at a time).

Back panel
• Place the hardboard for the back panel with the

smooth side up in the centre of the calico. Apply Bostik to the hardboard and glue the calico edge onto the back as described for the frame panel. Trim the excess fabric.

Bow
• Fold one long edge of the fabric for the band over to the wrong side three times, 2 cm at a time, press and glue each fold.
• Fold the pink fabric for the lower bow in half lengthways with the right sides together.
• Continue, following the rest of the instructions for the double bow of *Rectangular calico picture frame* on p. 8, but stitch through all layers parallel to the short sides 22 cm (instead of 13 cm) from the fold.

Finishing
• Cut the mirror tape squares in half. Glue two pieces in the centre at the back of the mirror and arrange the rest around the edge.
• Place the mirror on the wrong side of the back panel and press it down onto the mirror tape.
• Place the back panel on the back of the frame panel with the mirror down.
• On the back panel mark the positions for eight evenly spaced screws 1,5 cm from the edge. Carefully drill holes at the marks through the calico and hardboard and screw the panels together.
• In the back panel, 3 cm from the long edges and 3 cm from the top edge, carefully drill holes for the hooks for the chain, screw in the hooks and hook in the chain.
• With Bostik glue the bow into position (see photograph).

Rectangular floral mirror frame with lace frill *(24,5 cm × 36 cm)*

The corners of this mirror must be cut diagonally to be out of the way of the screws. Make a mark 4 cm from each corner and draw a line between the two points. Ask your dealer to cut the mirror along that line. Have the hardboard cut when you buy it. Draw the window (15,5 cm × 27 cm) on the hardboard and add a 4,5 cm edge all round. Place a round spice bottle on the corners of the frame, back panel and the window to obtain the correct curve.

MATERIALS

2-3 mm-thick mirror: 18 cm × 30 cm
3 mm-thick hardboard: 24,5 cm × 36 cm (2 pieces)
2 cm-thick foam: 24,5 cm × 36 cm
Floral fabric for frame panel: 34 cm × 45 cm; and back panel: 30 cm × 40 cm
Calico for frame panel: 34 cm × 45 cm

Pink cotton fabric for lower bow: 15 cm × 52 cm; and band for bow: 4 cm × 10 cm
Green fabric for top bow: 9 cm × 22 cm
2,5 cm-wide torchon lace for edge of window: 1 m
10 cm-wide cream anglaise lace with pink embroidery: 2,5 m
Pink cotton piping: 2,2 m
8 screws: 6 mm × 16 mm
2 screw-in hooks for chain
Chain: 20 cm
2 squares 2 mm-thick double-sided mirror tape
Clear adhesive (Bostik)
Hot-glue gun and glue sticks (optional)
Drill with 1,8 mm bit
Screwdriver

METHOD

• Saw or have the hardboard sawn for the frame and back panel (see p. 4).

Frame panel
• Cut out the foam following the frame panel using the Stanley knife.
• With Bostik glue the foam onto the rough side of the frame panel.
• Place the frame panel with the foam down in the centre of the calico. Apply Bostik at the back along the long

21

sides of the frame panel, fold the calico to the back and glue together. Repeat with the two short sides.
- Neatly glue the corners (see p. 5).
- Cut out the calico all round 3 cm from the window.
- Cut notches 2 cm apart in the calico edge around the window up to the cardboard edge. Press the calico and foam together along the edge where you are cutting.
- Apply Bostik to the back around the window. Fold the notched calico to the back section by section and glue together. Pay special attention to the corners.
- Cover the frame panel with the floral fabric in exactly the same way.
- With Bostik glue the torchon lace onto one half of the window edge so that one edge folds to the back. Glue the other half.
- Apply Bostik to the back around the window and glue the lace onto it.
- Cut a 70 cm piece of cotton piping and glue it at the back around the window.
- Glue the rest of the piping to the back along the outside edge of the frame panel.
- Trim the anglaise lace to a width of 5 cm and gather.
- Using a thick line of Bostik glue the anglaise frill section by section (± 20 cm at a time) onto the outside edge of the frame panel.

Back panel
- Cover the back panel with the cotton fabric in the same way as the frame panel. Apply the glue to the smooth side of the hardboard.

Double bow
- Fold one long edge of fabric for the band to the wrong side twice, 1 cm at a time, press and glue each fold.
- Fold the fabric for the lower bow in half lengthways with the right sides together. Stitch the edges together with a 0,5 cm seam allowance, but leave an opening in the long side to turn the strip right side out. Stitch the corners at a slight curve.
- Continue, following the rest of the instructions for the double bow of *Rectangular calico picture frame* on p. 8, but replace the taffeta with cotton fabric.

Finishing
- Cut the mirror tape squares in half and arrange the four pieces on the back of the mirror. Ensure that one piece is placed in the centre of the mirror.
- Place the mirror onto the back panel and press it down.
- Place the back panel with the mirror down onto the back of the frame panel.
- Mark the positions for the screws 1,5 cm from the edge: three holes evenly spaced on each long side and one in the centre of each short side.
- Carefully drill holes at the marks through the cotton fabric and hardboard and screw the panels together.
- Carefully drill holes, 3 cm from the long edges and 3 cm from the top edge, for the hooks for the chain in the back panel, screw in the hooks and hook in the chain.
- With Bostik glue the bow into position (see photograph).

Sewing basket

MATERIALS

Round basket with separate lid: 18 cm in diameter and ± 12 cm high
± 2 mm-thick cardboard: 18 cm × 18 cm
Batting: 18 cm × 18 cm
Pink floral cotton fabric for cover: 25 cm × 25 cm
Pink ticking for side of basket: 10 cm × 55 cm
Pink cotton fabric for bow: 12 cm × 60 cm; and band of bow: 3 cm × 4 cm
3 cm-wide torchon lace for cover: 42 cm
2 cm-wide torchon lace for side of cover: 55 cm
2,5 cm-wide cream anglaise lace with pink embroidery for basket: 55 cm
3 cm-wide cream anglaise lace with pink embroidery for lid frill: 1,5 m
Pink cotton piping: 54 cm
8 mm-wide pink ribbon: 1,2 m
Clear adhesive (Bostik)
Hot-glue gun and glue sticks (optional)
Wood glue
Stanley knife

METHOD

Lid
- Trace the outline of the lid onto the cardboard and cut out using a Stanley knife.
- Cut out the batting according to the cardboard.
- Place the cardboard on the floral fabric, add 2 cm all round and cut out.
- With Bostik glue the batting onto the cardboard.
- Place the cardboard with the batting down in the centre on the wrong side of the floral fabric. Apply Bostik to the edge of the cardboard, fold the fabric to the back and glue together. Make small folds in the fabric at the curves, if necessary.
- Fold the long edge of the fabric for the band to the wrong side twice, 1 cm at a time, press and glue each fold.
- Fold the fabric for the bow in half lengthways with the right sides together and stitch the long sides with a 0,5 cm seam allowance.
- Turn the strip right side out and press so that the seam lies next to the fold.
- Fold the strip in half with the short edges and the wrong sides together and stitch it with a 0,5 cm seam allowance.
- Fold the strip so that the seam is in the middle at the back.
- Gather the strip into three folds in the centre to form a bow.
- Place the band around the folds and stitch it at the back with a double thread of cotton. Trim the excess fabric.
- Apply Bostik to the back of the band and glue the bow to the centre of the covered cardboard (see photograph).

Fold the long ends of the bow around the cardboard edge and glue onto the back.
• Cut the 3 cm-wide torchon lace in half and with Bostik glue the two strips onto either side 0,5 cm from the bow (see photograph).
• Cut two 20 cm pieces of ribbon and with Bostik glue them on 0,5 cm from the inside edge of the torchon lace
• With Bostik glue the piping at the back along the edge of the covered cardboard.
• Gather the anglaise lace for the frill. Start at the same point as for the piping and with Bostik glue the gathered edge of the frill at the back along the piping on the edge. First glue one half and then the rest.
• Apply a zigzag strip of Bostik to the edge of the basket lid. Glue the torchon lace with one side flush with the lower edge of the lid. Fold the other edge over the top and glue it onto the top of the lid.
• Start at the edge of the cover and apply four circles of wood glue to the lid. Glue the trimmed, covered card-board onto the lid, place three heavy books on top and leave for ± 3 hours.

Basket
• Fold one long edge of the ticking 1 cm to the wrong side.
• Apply a zigzag strip of Bostik to the side of the basket and glue on the ticking with the folded edge at the bottom and the raw edge next to the top edge. Fold the short edge, which is glued last, 1 cm to the wrong side and glue.
• With Bostik glue the 2,5 cm-wide anglaise lace to the top edge of the basket. Ensure that the join corresponds with that of the ticking.
• Cut a 55 cm piece of ribbon and glue it to the top edge of the basket onto the anglaise lace. Ensure that the joins correspond.
• Tie the remaining ribbon in a bow and glue it to the end of the ribbon join.

23

Wedding album

MATERIALS

Album
Standard-size ten-page ring-back album
± 1 mm-thick cardboard for flyleaves: 22 cm × 28,5 cm
    (2 pieces)
Batting: 32 cm × 52 cm
Calico for cover: 34 cm × 58 cm; and flyleaves: 24 cm ×
    32 cm (2 pieces)
3 cm-wide cream anglaise lace for cover front and spine:
    1,6 m
2,5 cm-wide cream anglaise lace for frill: 2,5 m
3,5 cm-wide cream satin ribbon: 1,25 m
Cream satin piping: 1,65 m
Clear adhesive (Bostik)
Wood glue
Hot-glue gun and glue sticks (optional)

Frame
± 2 mm-thick cardboard: 19 cm × 22 cm
Batting: 19 cm × 22 cm (2 pieces)
Calico: 19 cm × 22 cm
3 cm-wide cream anglaise lace for frill: 2 m
1 cm-wide torchon lace for edge of window: 35 cm
1,5 cm-wide cream satin ribbon for rose: 1,25 m
Cream satin piping: 1,02 m
2 artificial leaves

METHOD

Cover
• With Bostik glue the batting onto the cover of the album and trim the edges.
• Open the album and place the cover with the batting down in the centre of the calico. Apply Bostik on the inside to the short sides of the cover, fold the fabric back and glue together.
• Repeat with the long sides, including the double layer at the corners.
• Cut two 25 cm strips and two 35 cm strips of anglaise lace for the cover front.
• With Bostik glue the lace first onto the two short sides and then onto the two long sides (see photograph). Trim the ends of the short lace strips flush with the edge. Fold the raw edges and the ends of the long lace strips to the inside and glue. Note that the raw edge of the lace along the long side next to the spine folds over onto the spine.
• Fold the raw edge of the anglaise lace for the spine 1 cm to the wrong side and with Bostik glue it to the spine so that the embroidered edge faces the cover front (see photograph).
• Glue the piping on the inside along the outside edge of the album. Start and finish in the centre of the lower edge of the spine.
• Gather the anglaise lace for the frill.
• Apply Bostik to the back of the piping along the outside edge. Glue the gathered edge of the lace to the pip-

ing section by section (see photograph). Start at the same point as for the piping.

Flyleaves
• Follow the instructions for the flyleaves of *Pink photo album for a teenager* on p. 6.

Frame
• Cut the frame panel (fig. 7a) out of the cardboard using the Stanley knife.
• With Bostik glue the batting onto one side (the front) of the frame panel.
• Place the remaining batting on top and trim the edges flush with the outside edge of the frame panel.
• Cut out the batting flush with the inside edge (at the window) of the frame panel.
• Place the frame panel with the batting down in the centre of the calico. Apply Bostik at the back to the outside edge of the frame panel.
• Press the cardboard down firmly onto the batting and calico with one hand by spreading five fingers evenly around the window edge. With the other hand fold the calico along one long edge to the back. Glue together.
• Repeat with the other long edge and then with the two short edges.
• Neatly glue the four corners (see p. 5).
• Push back with your finger any batting protruding beyond the edge of the window.
• Cut out the calico all round 1 cm from the window.
• Cut notches ± 1 cm apart up to the cardboard edge in the calico edge around the window. Push the batting back between the calico and the cardboard, pressing together where you are cutting.
• Apply Bostik at the back around the window. Fold the notched calico edge back section by section and glue together.
• Cut a 66 cm piece of satin piping.
• With Bostik glue it at the back along the outside edge of the frame panel.
• Cut notches ± 1 cm apart in one edge of the torchon lace.
• Apply a thin line of Bostik in front along one half of the window edge. Wipe off the excess glue towards the back with your finger, leaving only a very thin layer. Be very careful not to allow any glue to run to the front.
• Glue the torchon lace onto one half of the window edge so that the notched edge folds round to the back. Repeat with the other half.
• Apply Bostik at the back around the window and glue the notched edge of the torchon lace.
• Cut a 36 cm piece of satin piping and with Bostik glue it at the back onto the edge of the window.
• Gather the anglaise lace for the frill.
• Apply Bostik at the back to the piping along the outside edge and glue on the gathered edge of the lace frill section by section.
• Glue the frame to the front of the album (see photograph) with wood glue and place under a weight (e.g. two heavy books) for ± 3 hours to dry.
• Make a ribbon rose (see p. 5) and glue it and the artificial leaves into position with Bostik (see photograph).

Triple frame (for three postcard-size photographs)

MATERIALS

± 2 mm-thick cardboard for frame and back panel:
   14 cm × 17 cm (6 pieces)
Batting: 16 cm × 19 cm (3 pieces)
Calico for outer cover: 21 cm × 50 cm; frame panels:
   18 cm × 22 cm (3 pieces); joining strips: 4 cm ×
   19 cm (2 strips); and back panels: 11 cm × 14 cm
   (3 pieces)
4 cm-wide torchon lace for frame panels: 2,5 m
2 cm-wide torchon lace for frame panels: 2,5 cm
6 mm-wide cream satin ribbon for frame panels: 1,85 m
1 cm-wide cream satin ribbon for ribbon roses: 3 m
Cream satin piping: 1,5 m
6 artificial leaves
Clear adhesive (Bostik)
Wood glue
Hot-glue gun and glue sticks (optional)

Stanley knife

METHOD

Outer cover
• Place three pieces of cardboard 1 cm apart.
• Apply Bostik to the long sides of the piece of cardboard in the centre, and to the two long sides immediately adjacent to it.
• Glue the two calico joining strips onto the glued sides to join the three pieces of cardboard. Ensure that the pieces of cardboard do not shift.
• Apply a small amount of Bostik at the back to the top and bottom where the pieces of cardboard are joined. Fold over the ends of the calico strips and glue to the back.
• Place the three joined pieces of cardboard with the calico strips up on the 21 cm × 50 cm piece of calico. Ensure that the outside edge is the same distance from the edge of the fabric all round.
• Apply Bostik to the long sides (top and bottom), fold the calico to the inside and glue together.
• Apply Bostik to the two short sides, fold the corners of the calico in slightly, and glue the edge to the back.
• Apply Bostik to the cardboard next to the folded calico edge and glue a 9 cm × 11 cm piece of calico onto the inside of each piece of cardboard. Smooth the fabric with the fingers until taut.

Frame panel (make three)
• Draw lines parallel to and 4 cm from each side of a 14 cm × 17 cm piece of cardboard to determine the position of the window. Cut out the window using the Stanley knife.
• With Bostik glue a piece of batting onto one side (the front) of the frame panel. Trim the edges flush with the outside edge of the cardboard.
• Cut out the batting flush with the window.
• Place the frame panel with the batting down in the centre of a 20 cm × 22 cm piece of calico. Apply sufficient Bostik to the long sides.
• Press the cardboard down firmly on the batting and calico with one hand by spreading five fingers evenly around the window edge. With the other hand fold the calico along the long sides to the back. Glue together.
• Repeat with the two short sides. There will be three layers of calico at the corners.
• Cut out the calico 1,5 cm from the window all round.
• Cut notches ± 1 cm apart up to the cardboard edge in the calico edge around the window. Push the batting back between the calico and the cardboard, pressing together where you are cutting.
• Apply Bostik at the back around the window.
• Fold the notched calico edge of first the long sides and then the two short sides to the back and glue.
• Cut two 18 cm strips of wide lace and glue it in front onto the two short sides. Fold the ends to the back and glue. Carefully cut a small notch in the lace at each inside corner and press the lace down securely onto the edge of the window.

- Cut the remaining wide lace in half and glue it to the two long sides in the same way.
- Cut two 22 cm and two 18 cm pieces of narrow lace and glue it onto the wide lace around the window in the same way.
- Cut the ribbon into eight 8 cm pieces. Glue each ribbon onto the lace (see photograph) and glue the ends at the back.
- Cut two 14 cm and two 11 cm pieces of satin piping and glue it at the back onto the long and short window edges respectively.

Finishing
- Make three ribbon roses (see p. 5).
- Apply wood glue to the inside of the outer cover on the sides of the three sections. Note that the two outside photographs are inserted from the sides and the centre one from above. The relevant side is, therefore, not glued.
- Glue the three frame panels onto the inside of the outer cover and clamp with clothes-pegs for 3-4 hours.
- With Bostik glue the artificial leaves and ribbon roses onto the frame panels (see photograph).

Rectangular lace frame

(19,5 cm × 22,5 cm)

The frame is made of hardboard and filled with foam. Ask your dealer to saw the frame for you. First draw the window (9,5 cm × 12,5 cm) on the board and then add a 5 cm border all round. This will facilitate the sawing out of the window.

MATERIALS

Frame
3 mm-thick hardboard for frame and back panel:
    19,5 cm × 22,5 cm (2 pieces)
± 2 mm-thick cardboard: 1 cm × 22,5 cm (2 strips); and:
    1 cm × 17,5 cm
2 cm-thick foam: 25,5 cm × 28,5 cm
Calico for frame and back panel: 25,5 cm × 28,5 cm
    (2 pieces); and back panel: 13 cm × 16 cm
5 cm-wide torchon lace: 1,1 m
3 cm-wide torchon lace: 1,1 m
5 mm-wide cream satin ribbon: 1 m
Cream satin piping: 64 cm
Stanley knife
Clear adhesive (Bostik)
Wood glue
Hot-glue gun and glue sticks (optional)

Long cord
Calico for long cord: 15 cm × 38 cm; bow: 16 cm ×
    34 cm; and band for bow: 4 cm × 8 cm
5 mm-wide torchon lace: 70 cm

METHOD

- Have the hardboard sawn (or saw it yourself) as described above.

Frame panel
- Cut out foam according to the frame panel and glue with Bostik onto the rough side of the frame panel.
- Place the frame panel with the foam down in the centre of a 25,5 cm × 28,5 cm piece of calico. Apply sufficient Bostik to the long sides, fold the calico to the back and glue together.
- Repeat with the two short sides. There will be three layers of calico at the corners.
- Cut out the calico all round 2 cm from the window.
- Cut notches ± 2 cm apart up to the hardboard edge in the calico edge around the window. Press down the foam where you are cutting.
- Apply Bostik at the back around the window. Fold over the notched calico edge of the long sides and then the two short sides and glue to the back.
- Cut two 26 cm strips of wide lace and glue it in front onto the two short sides. Fold the ends to the back and glue. Carefully cut a small notch in the lace at each inside corner and press the lace down securely onto the window edge.
- Cut the remaining wide lace in half and glue it in front onto the two long sides in the same way.
- Cut two 28 cm and two 26 cm pieces of narrow lace and glue it onto the wide lace around the window in the same way.
- Cut the ribbon into eight equal pieces.
- Glue the ribbons onto the lace (see photograph) and glue the ends at the back.
- Cut two 18 cm and two 14 cm pieces of satin piping and glue it at the back onto the long and short window edges respectively.

Back panel
- With Bostik glue the 22,5 cm cardboard strips onto the smooth side along the long edges of the back panel. Glue the 17,5 cm strip onto the short side (bottom). The cardboard will provide sufficient space to insert the photograph easily.
- Place the outside of the back panel in the centre of the other 25,5 cm × 28,5 cm piece of calico. Apply Bostik to the edges, fold the fabric to the back and glue on as described for the frame panel.
- Round off the corners of the 13 cm × 16 cm piece of calico.
- Apply Bostik to the fabric edge on the back of the back panel. Glue on the 13 cm × 16 cm piece of calico. Smooth the fabric with the fingers until taut.
- Apply wood glue to the cardboard strips at the lower edge and the two side edges of the back panel, glue on the frame panel and clamp with clothes pegs for ± 3 hours.

Long cord
- Follow the instructions for the long cord of *Frames-on-a-cord* on p. 10.

± 1 mm-thick cardboard for flyleaves: 22 cm × 28,5 cm (2 pieces)
Batting: 32 cm × 52 cm
Calico for cover: 34 cm × 58 cm; and flyleaves: 24 cm × 32 cm (2 pieces)
Cream taffeta for bow: 18 cm × 40 cm; band for bow: 8 cm × 15 cm; for back: 6 cm × 35 cm
Variety of torchon lace of different widths, textures and shades to decorate the cover front (see photograph): 10-42 cm long (16 strips)
2 cm-wide cream anglaise lace for spine: 35 cm
6 mm-wide cream satin ribbon to decorate cover front: ± 70 cm
8 mm-wide cream satin ribbon to decorate cover front: ± 70 cm
3,5 cm-wide cream satin ribbon to tie album: 1,25 m
Clear adhesive (Bostik)
Wood glue
Hot-glue gun and glue sticks (optional)

METHOD

Cover
• With Bostik glue the batting onto the cover of the album and trim the edges.
• Open the album and place the cover with the batting down in the centre of the calico. Apply Bostik on the inside to the short sides of the cover, fold the calico to the back and glue on the inside.
• Repeat with the long sides, including the double layer at the corners.
• Trim the cover front with torchon lace and ribbon as preferred or as in the photograph. Glue on the lace and ribbon.
• Glue the anglaise lace with the raw edge onto the spine of the album and the embroidered edge onto the cover front (see photograph).
• Fold the long raw edges of the taffeta strip for the back 0,5 cm to the wrong side and glue the strip onto the back. Fold the ends to the inside and glue.

Flyleaves
• Make the flyleaves and glue them into position with the ribbons, following the instructions for the flyleaves of *Pink photo album for a teenager* on p. 6.

Taffeta bow
• Fold one long edge of the fabric for the band over to the wrong side three times, 2 cm at a time, press and with Bostik glue each fold.
• Complete the rest of the bow following the instructions for the calico bow of *Rectangular lace frame* above. Remember to fold the taffeta strip for the bow in half lengthways with the right sides together.
• Apply Bostik to the back of the band and glue the bow into position on the cover front next to the spine (see photograph).

• Glue or stitch the lace onto the wrong side along the edge of the cord (see photograph)

Calico bow
• Follow the instructions for the single bow of *Frames-on-a-cord* on p. 10.

Finishing
• With Bostik glue the bow onto the long cord (see photograph).
• With Bostik glue the frame onto the band.
• Hook the top end of the band over a picture hook to hang.

Lace album

MATERIALS

Standard-size ten-page ring-back photo album

Diary

MATERIALS

Size A5 diary
Batting: 22 cm × 31 cm
Calico: 25 cm × 38 cm
Navy-blue fabric for front page: 10 cm × 25 cm
  (2 pieces); and band for bow: 3 cm × 4 cm
Wine-red fabric for bow: 10 cm × 20 cm
3 cm-wide cream anglaise lace: 50 cm
1 cm-wide cream anglaise lace: 50 cm
Clear adhesive (Bostik)
Hot-glue gun and glue sticks (optional)

METHOD

• With Bostik glue the batting onto the cover and trim the edges.
• Fold open the book and place the cover with the batting down in the centre of the calico. Apply Bostik on the inside along the short sides of the cover, fold the calico to the back and glue together. Loosen the bound pages slightly at the top and bottom of the spine to push the fabric underneath.
• Apply Bostik to the full length of the long edges, fold the fabric to the back and glue together, including the double layer at the corners.
• Fold the long raw edges of each navy fabric strip 1 cm to the wrong side and iron the folds.
• Cut the 3 cm-wide anglaise lace in half and fold the raw edge 0,5 cm to the wrong side. Place the anglaise lace with the folded edge 0,5 cm from one long edge of each navy fabric strip and stitch (or glue) on.
• Cut the 1 cm-wide anglaise lace in half. Glue with the right side up onto the wrong side of each fabric edge where the wide anglaise lace has been stitched or glued.
• Place the lace-decorated edges of the two fabric strips 3,5 cm apart on the cover front (see figure and photograph).
• Apply Bostik to the wrong side of one navy-blue fabric strip (outer strip) and glue together. Apply Bostik on the inside along the edge of the cover front and fold the fabric to the inside. Glue the two short sides first and then the long side.
• Fold the long raw edge of the other navy-blue strip 0,5 cm to the wrong side and glue it into position in the same way next to the spine on the cover front.
• Glue the first and last pages of the book to the inside of the cover as flyleaves to conceal the raw edges of the folded fabric.

Bow

• Fold one long edge of the navy-blue fabric for the band over to the wrong side twice, 2 cm at a time, press and glue each fold with Bostik.
• Continue, following the rest of the instructions for the single bow of *Frames-on-a-cord* on p. 10, but replace the calico with wine-red fabric.

• Apply Bostik at the back to the stitched section of the band and glue the bow into position on the cover front (see photograph).

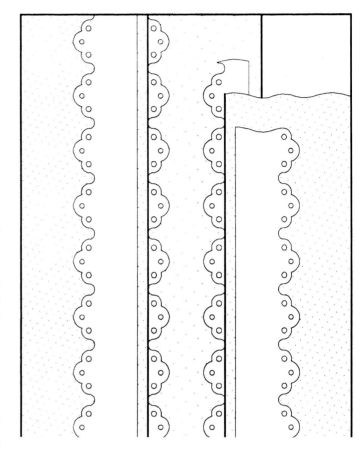

Fig. 4

Telephone/address index book

MATERIALS

Hard-cover telephone/address index book: 10,5 cm × 14,5 cm
Thin batting: 15 cm × 21 cm
Floral fabric: 17 cm × 25 cm
Maroon fabric for spine: 6,8 cm × 17 cm; and corner: 8 cm × 15 cm
2 cm-wide cream anglaise lace: 34 cm
6 mm-wide cream ribbon: 34 cm
Clear adhesive (Bostik)

METHOD

• With Bostik glue the batting onto the cover and trim the edges.

• Fold open the book and place the cover with the batting down in the centre on the wrong side of the floral fabric. Apply Bostik on the inside along the short sides of the cover, fold the fabric to the back and glue together. Slightly loosen the bound pages at the top and bottom of the spine to push the fabric underneath.

• Apply Bostik along the full length of the long edges, fold the fabric to the back and glue together, including the double layer at the corners.

• Apply Bostik to the spine and glue the maroon strip onto it. Fold the top and bottom ends of the fabric to the inside and glue.

• Cut the lace in half and glue it along either side of the maroon strip with the raw edge next to the long raw edge of the maroon strip. Fold the ends to the inside and glue.

• Cut the ribbon in half and glue it to the raw edges where the lace and the maroon strip meet.

• Fold one long edge of the maroon fabric for the corner 1 cm to the wrong side.

• Place the centre of the long raw edge exactly at the corner so that the strip lies diagonally across the corner (see photograph). Apply Bostik to the maroon fabric and glue together.

• Glue the first and last pages of the book to the inside of the cover as flyleaves to hide the raw edges of the fabric.

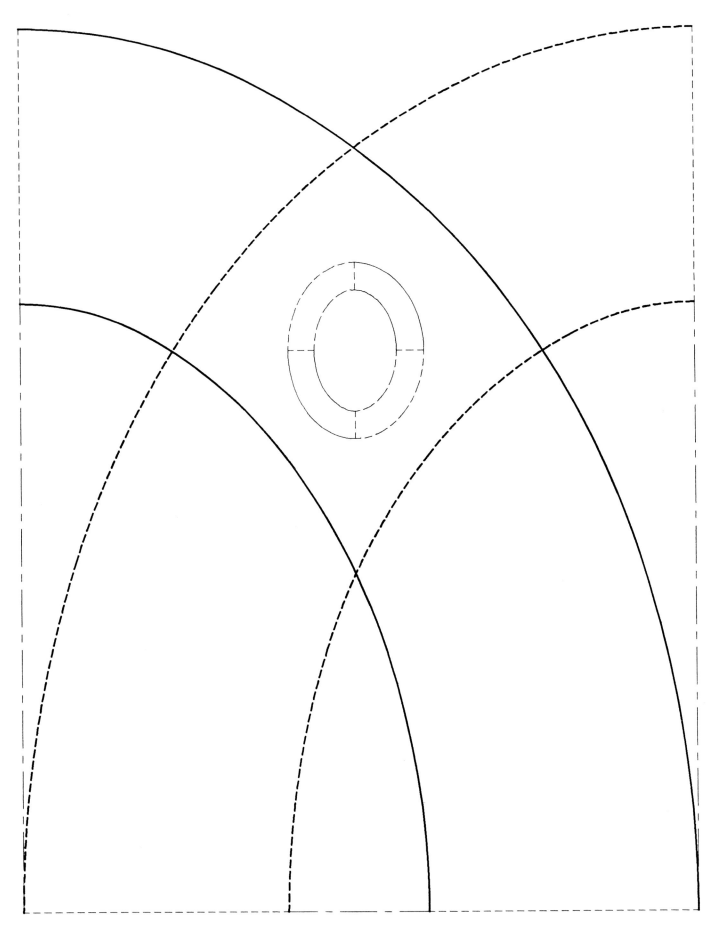

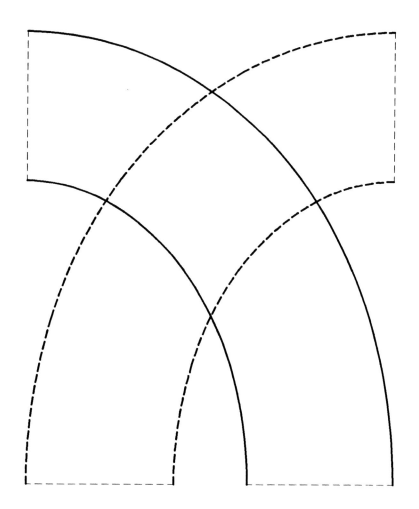

Fig. 6
Small, oval-shaped calico frame (p. 13)

Fig. 5 (left)
Large, oval-shaped mirror frame with calico frill (p. 12)
Oval-shaped mirror with floral frame (p. 20)

31

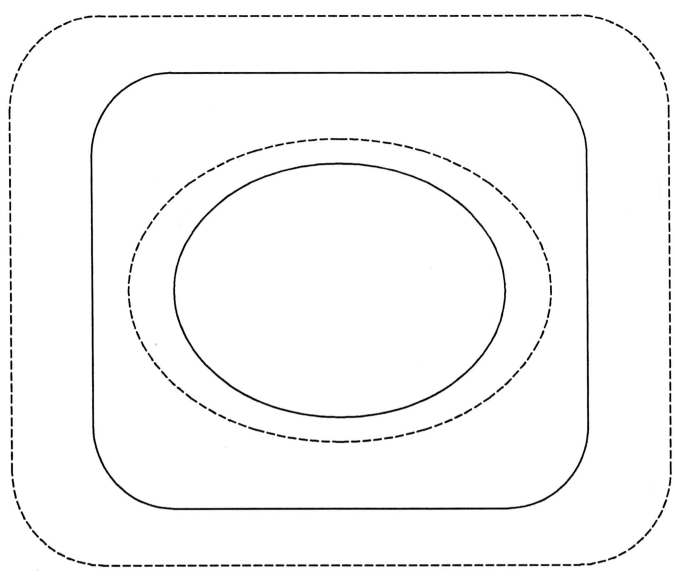

Fig. 7a
Pink photo album for a teenager (p. 6): Follow solid line
Frames-on-a-cord (p. 9): Follow solid line
Small upright frame (p. 18): Follow solid line
Large upright frame (p. 19): Follow broken line
Wedding album (p. 24): Follow broken line

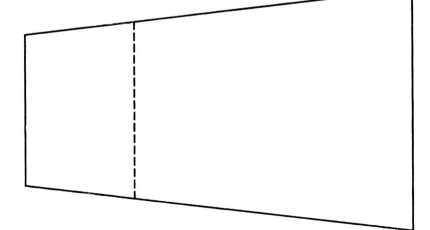

Fig. 7b
Support